Chris Colfer

Gillian Gosman

PowerKiDS press.

New York

Published in 2012 by The Rosen Publishing Group, Inc.
29 East 21st Street, New York, NY 10010

First Edition

Editor: Jennifer Way
Book Design: Kate Laczynski
Layout Design: Julio Gil

Photo Credits: Cover Larry Busacca/Getty Images for EJAF; p. 4 Lester Cohen/WireImage/Getty Images; p. 7 Mitch Haddad/ABC via Getty Images; p. 8 Clinton Gilders/FilmMagic/Getty Images; p. 11 Barry Brecheisen/Getty Images for Fox; p. 12 Ray Tamarra/Getty Images; pp. 15, 16 Kevin Winter/Getty Images; p. 19 Bob Levey/Getty Images for Fox; p. 20 Jason Merritt/Getty Images.

Library of Congress Cataloging-in-Publication Data

Gosman, Gillian.
Chris Colfer / by Gillian Gosman. — 1st ed.
    p. cm. — (Kid stars!)
Includes webliography and index.
ISBN 978-1-4488-6193-4 (library binding) — ISBN 978-1-4488-6347-1 (pbk.) —
ISBN 978-1-4488-6348-8 (6-pack)
1. Colfer, Chris, 1990-—Juvenile literature. 2. Actors—United States—Biography—Juvenile literature. 3. Singers—United States—Biography—Juvenile literature. I. Title.
PN2287.C5698G67 2012
791.4302'8092—dc23
[B]
                                                              2011029671

Manufactured in the United States of America

CPSIA Compliance Information: Batch #WW12PK: For Further Information contact Rosen Publishing, New York, New York at 1-800-237-9932

Contents

Meet Chris Colfer 5

Young Chris 6

Getting Started 9

Kurt Hummel 10

Glee 13

And the Winner Is... 14

The Golden Globes 17

The Write Stuff 18

Colfer Offscreen 21

Fun Facts 22

Glossary 23

Index 24

Web Sites 24

Glee was an immediate, award-winning hit that made stars of its cast. Chris Colfer, who plays Kurt Hummel on the show, is shown here at the 2011 People's Choice Awards.

Meet Chris Colfer

Chris Colfer has told fans that his first word as a baby was "Oprah," the superstar of television and film and one of Chris's personal heroes. He has been thinking of a stage and screen career ever since. It has been clear since Chris was very young that he had talent. He also had a tough time at school facing the **bullies** who picked on him for being different.

Luckily for Chris and for his fans, he has found a place to show his talent and help young people like him. That place is television's smash hit *Glee*.

Young Chris

Christopher Paul Colfer was born on May 27, 1990, in Clovis, California. Clovis is a small city in the center of the state.

Chris was involved in many creative activities growing up. At Clovis East High School, he joined the speech and debate club and the drama club. He was president of the school's Writers' Club and in charge of the school's **literary magazine**. As a young man, he acted onstage in community theater shows. In 2008, when he was a senior in high school, he wrote, directed, and starred in *Shirley Todd*. This was a **spoof** of the musical *Sweeney Todd*.

Colfer sometimes appears on talk shows to help promote *Glee*. Here he is on *Jimmy Kimmel Live* in 2011.

The *Glee* cast has gone on tour to perform songs from the show. From left to right are Chris Colfer, Amber Riley, Jenna Ushkowitz, and Lea Michele.

In 2009, Colfer starred in a short film called *Russel Fish: The Sausage and Eggs **Incident***. The movie tells the story of Russel Fish, a brainy young man who has to pass a test in gym class or fail. If he fails gym, he will lose his place at Harvard University. With the help of his best friend, Russel passes the test, proving the mean gym teacher and the bullies wrong.

Russel Fish: The Sausage and Eggs Incident was shown at **film festivals**. It won awards for short films. This short film helped Colfer get noticed for other acting projects. Starring in a short film helped put him on the path toward stardom.

 Kurt Hummel

In 2009, Colfer **auditioned** for *Glee*. The show was to be about the students in a high-school glee club, or singing group. Colfer auditioned for the role of Artie Abrams. He was cast on the show but not as Artie.

Ryan Murphy, the show's creator, had liked Colfer's singing and acting so much that he decided to write a new role just for him. Colfer would play the part of Kurt Hummel, a member of the glee club who stays true to himself even when he is bullied for being different.

Kevin McHale (right) was cast in the role of Artie Abrams, the role for which Colfer (center) auditioned. On the left is Dianna Agron, who plays Quinn Fabray on *Glee*.

The *Glee* cast filmed part of the last episode of the second season in New York City's Central Park. Colfer's character, Kurt, (right) is known for his bold fashion sense. Colfer says that he is sometimes surprised by his character's clothing choices!

Glee

The first episode of *Glee* aired in the United States on May 19, 2009. The show was so popular that is soon was shown around the world, in countries including Canada, Australia, New Zealand, South Africa, Brazil, Great Britain, Italy, Lithuania, Ireland, the Philippines, India, Malaysia, Japan, Indonesia, Singapore, and the island of Fiji!

The fans of *Glee* are called Gleeks, a mix of the words "glee" and "geek." "Geek" is usually used as an insult, but *Glee* fans use the word differently. They use it to show they are happy to be themselves, even if that means being seen as weird by others. This is one of the major themes, or main ideas, of the show.

And the Winner Is...

Glee and its cast, including Chris Colfer, have been **nominated** and won Emmy Awards, Golden Globe Awards, a Peabody Award, Screen Actors Guild Awards, and People's Choice Awards. The songs performed by Colfer and the *Glee* cast have become fast-selling downloads on iTunes, and the sound track albums of songs sung on the show have been best sellers.

Colfer and the rest of the *Glee* cast have performed for President Obama at the White House. They have been guests on *Oprah*. They sang the **national anthem** at the World Series. They have performed across the country in a sold-out concert tour.

The *Glee* cast performed the opening song at the sixty-second Emmy Awards, in 2010. The show won three Emmys that year.

Audiences were moved by the way Colfer showed Kurt dealing with being bullied as well as his powerful singing voice. Here he is after winning a Golden Globe in 2011.

The Golden Globes

In 2011, Colfer won the Golden Globe for the Best Performance by a **Supporting Actor**. At the age of 20, he became the youngest person ever to receive this award!

When he accepted his Golden Globe, he gave a speech that touched many people. He said thank you to "all the amazing kids that watch our show and that our show celebrates and are constantly told 'no' [by] people and environments and bullies at school, that they can't be who they are or can't have what they want because of who they are." This speech became a popular clip on YouTube, where more than one million people watched it!

The Write Stuff

   Glee's creator has said that Kurt Hummel will graduate from, or leave, William McKinley High School at the end of *Glee*'s third season, in 2012. Colfer tells fans not to worry, though. That likely will not be the end of his time playing Kurt.

   While he spends a lot of time working on the *Glee* set, Colfer has also become a writer. In 2012, an adventure **novel** written by Colfer called *The Land of Stories* hit the stores, and he plans to keep writing books. He has also written a movie called *Struck by Lightning*.

Colfer (right) and other *Glee* cast members sign autographs for Gleeks, or fans of the show, when the show goes on tour.

Glee will be Colfer's main project through 2012. He has writing and acting projects waiting in the wings, though!

Colfer Offscreen

Colfer has many projects that he is working on during his breaks from filming *Glee*. He is writing a television show for the Disney Channel called *The Little Leftover Witch*. The show is based on the book of the same name by Florence Laughlin. It tells the story of a young witch who joins a friendly family after her broom crashes nearby.

Colfer also gives his time to help people in need. He has worked for Education Through Music, a group that brings music to students in schools that do not have music classes.

FUN FACTS

 Colfer was chosen as one of the *Time* 100, a list of the most important people of 2011 created by *Time* magazine.

 In high school, Chris won state championships, or awards, for speech and debate.

His favorite actor is Kristin Chenoweth. She is a Broadway actor who guest stars as April Rhodes on *Glee*.

 Glee fans love the show's sound tracks. Two of the sound tracks have sold more than 500,000 copies, and two have sold more than one million copies!

 When he was little, Chris's favorite movie was *Sister Act*.

When he auditioned for *Glee*, Colfer had been a college student for two weeks. On the weekends, he worked behind the counter at a dry cleaner. His simple life was about to change forever!

 Colfer has a scar on the left side of his neck from an operation.

 Colfer loves Disneyland!

 Chris's first time on stage was in a grade-school production of *You're a Good Man, Charlie Brown*. He played the role of Snoopy!

 Colfer knows how to use a sai sword, a Japanese weapon!

Glossary

auditioned (ah-DIH-shund) Tried out.

bullies (BU-leez) People who are mean to others and try to make them feel bad about themselves.

film festivals (FILM FES-tuh-vulz) Events at which films are shown in different theaters in one city.

incident (IN-sih-dent) Something that happens.

literary magazine (LIH-teh-rer-ee MA-guh-zeen) A publication that has stories, poetry, and essays among other things related to literature.

national anthem (NASH-nul ANT-them) A country's official song.

nominated (NO-muh-nayt-ed) Suggested that someone or something should be given an award or a position.

novel (NAH-vul) A long story about made-up people and events.

spoof (SPOOF) Something that pokes fun at another work in a light, funny way.

supporting actor (suh-PAWRT-ing AK-tur) Someone who has a part in a play, film, or show that is not a lead part.

Index

B
bullies, 5, 9, 17

C
club, 6, 10
community theater
  shows, 6

E
Emmy Awards, 14

F
fans, 5, 13, 18, 22
film festivals, 9

G
Glee, 5, 10, 13–14,
  21–22

H
heroes, 5

L
literary magazine, 6

N
national anthem, 14
novel, 18

S
spoof, 6
superstar, 5

Web Sites

Due to the changing nature of Internet links, PowerKids Press has developed an online list of Web sites related to the subject of this book. This site is updated regularly. Please use this link to access the list:
www.powerkidslinks.com/kids/colfer/